MATH SERIES

ADVANCED
ADDITION

by S. Harold Collins

Book design by Kathy Kifer.

Copyright © 1987 by Stanley H. Collins

Published by:
Garlic Press
605 Powers St.
Eugene, OR 97402

ISBN 978-0-931993-15-2
Order Number GP-015
Printed in China

www.garlicpress.com

To Parents and Teachers,

The Advanced Straight Forward Math Series has been designed for parents and teachers of children. This is the addition book. It is a straightforward, sequenced presentation of advanced addition skills. It assumes that basic addition facts have already been learned (if not, consult our first series: **The Straight Forward Math Series**).

These steps are suggested for mastery of advanced addition skills:

- Give the **Basic Facts Review** (page 1) to assure competency in basic addition facts. The test has 100 problems and is arranged to group facts (see Answers, page 28, for a display of facts).

  If knowledge of Basic Facts is not demonstrated, do not go on to the next level. Master Basic Facts first, they are crucial to addition success in this advanced series.

- Give the **Beginning Assessment Test** to determine where to start Practice Sheets. The Beginning Assessment Test (page 2) will tell which advanced addition skills are sound and which need attention. Begin Practice Sheets where the Beginning Assessment Test shows that addition errors start.

  Look at the Beginning Assessment Test. If you consult the Answers on page 28, you will see that the problems are arranged in groupings. Each grouping is a skill. Each skill is essential and requires mastery before a higher skill is started.

- Start **Practice Sheets** at the appropriate skill level as determined from the Beginning Assessment Test. Do not skip levels once begun; build to mastery of all skills.

  Practice Sheets are given for each skill level to provide ample practice.

  Set a standard to move from one addition level to the next, either a percentage correct or a number correct.

- Give **Review Sheets** after completion of each section.

- Give **Section Diagnostic Test** as a final measure of a particular section. Section Diagnostic Tests are arranged to identify problems which may still exist with a particular skill (much like the Beginning Assessment Test).

  Set a standard to move from one section to the next. If that standard is not met, go back, focus on problem skills with Practice Sheets or similar materials.

- Give the **Final Assessment Test** to measure all advanced addition skills. Compare change from the Beginning Assessment Test.

Table of Contents

Basic Facts Review

0 + 9	9 + 8	6 + 7	5 + 4	1 + 3	0 + 2	2 + 1	9 + 0	3 + 0	5 +10
9 + 6	1 + 9	7 + 8	3 + 7	9 + 4	4 + 3	5 + 2	4 + 1	8 + 0	1 + 0
4 + 5	8 + 6	2 + 9	6 + 8	1 + 7	4 + 4	5 + 3	3 + 2	8 + 1	7 + 0
10 + 4	2 + 5	7 + 6	3 + 9	5 + 8	8 + 7	7 + 4	6 + 3	6 + 2	3 + 1
0 + 0	2 + 4	9 + 5	10 + 6	4 + 9	4 + 8	2 + 7	8 + 4	2 + 3	7 + 2
8 + 8	3 + 3	8 + 4	6 + 5	4 + 6	5 + 9	3 + 8	9 + 7	5 + 4	8 + 3
7 + 3	1 + 1	6 + 6	7 + 4	3 + 5	3 + 6	6 + 9	2 + 8	10 + 7	2 + 4
8 + 2	5 + 3	2 + 2	9 + 9	3 + 4	8 + 5	2 + 6	7 + 9	1 + 8	5 + 7
0 +10	9 + 2	10 + 3	5 + 5	10 + 10	1 + 4	1 + 5	1 + 6	8 + 9	0 + 8
9 + 10	8 + 10	10 + 2	0 + 3	4 + 4	7 + 7	0 + 4	7 + 5	0 + 6	9 + 9

Beginning Assessment Test

4	2	6	1	5	8	4
4	6	0	2	7	3	9
+ 1	+ 2	+ 3	+ 5	+ 2	+ 6	+ 6

52	11	56	70	24	23	35
+ 24	+ 82	+ 43	+ 19	+ 24	11	23
					+ 33	+ 11

417	513	942	417	523	713	224
+ 72	+ 64	+ 30	40	23	46	132
			+ 31	+ 23	+ 30	+ 111

35	88	28	44	47	19	18
+ 7	+ 2	+ 9	+ 8	+ 6	+ 27	+ 25

68	94	64	46	53	17	67
+ 54	+ 96	+ 36	+ 85	28	28	64
				+ 15	+ 18	+ 69

440	278	509	594	394	386	472
+ 39	+ 19	+ 99	+ 186	+ 575	+ 239	+668

2,468	1,327	28,097	5,547,606
+ 1,912	+ 9,857	+ 11,646	+ 7,568,705

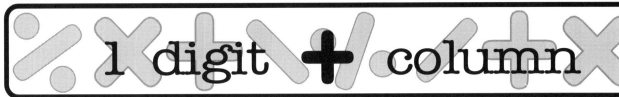

1 digit + column

sum 10 or less

```
   1        4        3        2        1        1        3
   7        4        4        2        0        6        3
 + 1      + 0      + 2      + 5      + 2      + 3      + 2
```

```
   4        1        1        2        4        2        5
   2        2        0        2        0        1        3
 + 1      + 3      + 9      + 1      + 3      + 1      + 1
```

```
   2        1        7        2        1        3        4
   2        0        2        0        5        3        2
 + 2      + 1      + 1      + 8      + 1      + 3      + 2
```

```
   5        4        1        2        0        7        2
   2        4        1        1        0        1        7
 + 3      + 0      + 1      + 4      + 0      + 1      + 1
```

```
   4        1        1        6        1        3        2
   4        2        1        0        1        3        1
 + 1      + 5      + 8      + 3      + 2      + 4      + 3
```

```
   5        3        2        6        1        2        3
   5        3        4        2        2        2        2
 + 0      + 3      + 1      + 2      + 5      + 6      + 5
```

```
   1        3        4        3        2        4        1
   7        1        2        2        6        4        2
 + 2      + 4      + 3      + 3      + 2      + 2      + 3
```

3

1 digit + column

sum greater than 10

4 1 +7	0 8 +8	4 4 +5	5 3 +9	2 3 +6	3 6 +9	2 5 +5
0 9 +7	7 6 +5	3 1 +9	6 3 +6	2 6 +8	3 3 +9	8 2 +3
1 8 +7	1 4 +8	2 7 +2	9 1 +9	7 4 +6	7 6 +5	6 4 +5
6 1 +8	3 3 +9	7 2 +8	5 4 +3	3 6 +5	3 6 +2	4 4 +5
5 3 +3	7 2 +7	4 4 +4	5 6 +7	9 7 +3	5 5 +6	7 7 +5
8 2 +4	3 8 +7	4 9 +6	2 7 +5	4 4 +4	8 3 +6	3 5 +4
7 4 +8	6 6 +6	5 5 +5	5 7 +7	6 5 +3	3 6 +9	4 9 +0

2 digits + 2 digits

no regrouping

21 + 32	12 + 17	32 + 46	18 + 21	37 + 51	30 + 40	24 + 53
33 + 24	82 + 17	62 + 20	41 + 17	23 + 13	42 + 34	11 + 22
62 + 27	53 + 41	13 + 45	44 + 35	27 + 60	54 + 32	21 + 17
11 + 16	10 + 72	32 + 61	34 + 43	66 + 13	22 + 23	16 + 12
31 + 21	51 + 16	44 + 44	15 + 24	36 + 63	47 + 12	55 + 14
27 + 22	15 + 24	17 + 82	33 + 33	11 + 44	10 + 40	32 + 37
45 + 44	12 13	61 + 10	22 + 22	19 + 20	82 + 17	41 + 51

2 digits + 2 digits

no regrouping

50 + 42	72 + 27	54 + 34	15 + 12	22 + 31	24 + 11	26 + 32
71 + 18	25 + 21	15 + 64	53 + 45	13 + 63	34 + 44	51 + 28
60 + 20	56 + 23	23 + 22	34 + 11	43 + 20	51 + 36	42 + 34
67 + 10	57 + 22	24 + 24	33 + 33	65 + 21	31 + 30	57 + 31
11 + 82	44 + 14	17 + 32	22 + 63	51 + 41	56 + 43	21 + 15
72 + 17	22 + 63	41 + 18	37 + 41	80 + 19	23 + 14	12 + 16
33 + 44	52 + 24	22 + 31	17 + 32	46 + 12	60 + 28	38 + 51

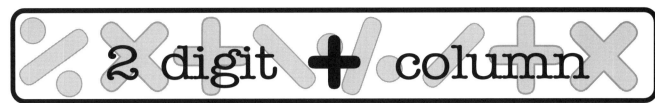

2 digit + column

no regrouping

46	11	10	21	13	21	43
31	23	52	46	13	30	15
+ 12	+ 34	+26	+ 12	+13	+ 45	+ 20

22	33	78	16	12	33	11
22	22	10	11	21	34	12
+ 22	+ 11	+ 11	+ 42	+ 12	+ 12	+ 13

44	22	31	31	13	23	23
33	23	32	14	31	31	22
+ 11	+ 24	+ 33	+ 34	+ 44	+ 43	+ 22

24	43	42	44	33	15	35
32	23	15	22	33	30	42
+ 11	+ 31	+ 21	+ 13	+ 33	+ 22	+ 11

12	43	15	51	35	61	12
13	22	12	22	11	23	16
+ 14	+ 13	+ 72	+ 24	+ 32	+ 15	+ 21

23	31	21	31	25	16	22
53	41	24	17	12	21	33
+ 11	+ 10	+ 31	+ 51	+ 12	+ 31	+ 41

34	11	23	12	21	70	35
12	15	11	73	22	15	23
+ 31	+ 20	+ 33	+ 14	+ 23	+ 12	+ 11

2 digit + column

no regrouping

43	54	16	13	33	51	12
30	12	22	22	32	24	23
+ 14	+ 12	+ 31	+ 31	+ 34	+ 22	+ 34

22	31	11	24	13	14	23
22	32	15	12	21	14	42
+ 23	+ 33	+ 42	+ 32	+ 41	+ 71	+ 24

27	15	22	11	33	42	51
11	51	21	21	33	43	35
+ 40	+ 13	+ 25	+ 57	+ 32	+ 11	+ 13

13	22	33	12	54	24	11
14	22	22	12	12	62	52
+ 22	+ 11	+ 42	+ 12	+ 32	+ 13	+ 31

24	21	11	25	24	44	44
12	34	35	31	12	13	21
+ 31	+ 41	+ 31	+ 13	+ 22	+ 21	+ 14

15	13	36	12	31	15	62
72	72	43	14	34	11	14
+ 12	+ 13	+ 10	+ 12	+ 24	+ 13	+ 13

24	43	23	11	33	41	12
33	22	22	12	13	42	17
+ 10	+ 32	+ 22	+ 26	+ 41	+ 14	+ 50

3 digits + 2 digits

no regrouping

122 + 73	140 + 30	12 + 603	744 + 35	422 + 72	444 + 45	217 + 62
223 + 75	424 + 62	336 + 43	51 + 618	573 + 25	423 + 44	219 + 60
252 + 37	624 + 44	366 + 33	217 + 62	112 + 77	169 + 30	83 + 614
365 + 24	580 + 18	107 + 42	122 + 77	281 + 18	707 + 92	378 + 21
114 + 54	222 + 55	323 + 56	942 + 30	503 + 92	27 + 852	832 + 32
122 + 77	24 + 603	885 + 14	822 + 76	111 + 86	215 + 73	333 + 55
912 + 67	704 + 92	627 + 72	513 + 64	219 + 80	20 + 472	313 + 16

3 digit + 2 digit

column, no regrouping

```
  312      101      273      413      521      610      728
   43       72       12       34       46       55       50
 + 31     + 26     + 13     + 30     + 21     + 20     + 11
```

```
  823      312      402      731      811      470      222
   34       70       60       23       33       15       33
 + 42     + 16     + 16     + 45     + 33     + 13     + 40
```

```
  121      510      337      800      924      647      411
   42       27       40       72       15       21       22
 + 20     + 31     + 20     + 26     + 60     + 31     + 44
```

```
  713      144      700      111      607      333      234
   46       44       50       23       41       41       45
 + 30     + 10     + 20     + 45     + 10     + 14     + 20
```

```
  823      101      243      112      970      416      523
   42       52       22       21       17       32       23
 + 11     + 15     + 13     + 42     + 10     + 40     + 23
```

```
  444      632      744      555      111      343      251
   22       32       32       20       44       34       23
 + 11     + 32     + 10     + 10     + 33     + 21     + 15
```

```
  222      732      334      417      213      401      525
   33       41       21       40       13       43       52
 + 44     + 15     + 33     + 31     + 13     + 51     + 11
```

3 digit + 3 digit

column, no regrouping

312	535	144	412	142	224	613
213	342	222	173	115	211	251
+ 114	+ 111	+ 213	+ 214	+ 121	+ 223	+ 132

361	253	314	751	213	535	443
423	113	372	122	312	211	322
+ 115	+ 132	+ 312	+ 124	+ 421	+ 132	+ 112

316	123	131	521	131	260	312
121	403	417	224	641	132	416
+ 231	+ 450	+ 251	+ 251	+ 123	+ 407	+ 121

224	134	222	324	315	146	221
332	412	233	433	312	212	422
+ 413	+ 131	+ 241	+ 130	+ 372	+ 320	+ 236

521	213	323	212	632	410	132
345	424	320	142	151	200	114
+ 102	+ 262	+ 125	+ 233	+ 112	+ 387	+ 141

413	531	313	224	623	123	343
410	214	331	132	231	222	323
+ 126	+ 234	+ 144	+ 111	+ 143	+ 322	+ 331

201	625	241	303	222	423	671
374	151	342	592	333	153	217
+ 121	+ 122	+ 116	+ 100	+ 444	+ 211	+ 101

Review Sheet

no regrouping

```
   6        3        4        4        2        4        2
   0        1        2        4        1        4        6
 + 3      + 4      + 3      + 2      + 4      + 1      + 2


   7        3        4        8        4        7        5
   4        8        4        3        9        7        3
 + 8      + 7      + 4      + 6      + 0      + 5      + 3


  15       17       11       44       34       22       16
+ 24     + 82     + 44     + 44     + 43     + 23     + 12


  23       43       61       11       12       24       22
  53       22       23       15       73       12       21
+ 11     + 13     + 15     + 20     + 14     + 31     + 25


 122      885       30      707      614      252      953
+ 77     + 12     + 942    + 92     + 63     + 37     + 36


 334      632      444      112      970      713      501
  21       32       22       21       17       46       62
+ 33     + 32     + 11     + 42     + 10     + 30     + 35


 213      212      123      303      531      134      307
 424      142      222      592      214      412      360
+262     +233     +222     +100     +234     +131     +231
```

Section
Diagnostic Test
no regrouping

2	4	2	4	8	9	8
1	4	6	4	3	4	7
+ 4	+ 1	+ 2	+ 4	+ 6	+ 5	+ 4

50	25	17	46	60	51	56
+ 42	+ 21	+ 32	+ 12	+ 28	+ 41	+ 43

36	12	33	12	24	22	11
43	14	22	12	62	22	35
+ 10	+ 12	+ 42	+ 12	+ 13	+ 11	+ 31

912	86	503	323	472	313	
+ 67	+111	+ 92	+ 56	+ 20	+ 16	

800	222	111	823	711	728	
72	33	23	34	33	50	
+ 26	+ 43	+ 45	+ 42	+ 33	+ 11	

213	134	314	613	146	324	
424	412	372	251	212	433	
+ 262	+ 131	+ 312	+ 132	+ 320	+ 130	

2 digits + 1 digit

regrouping

18 + 4	29 + 4	19 + 7	15 + 5	46 + 8	12 + 9	35 + 9
33 + 8	16 + 6	25 + 8	13 + 7	38 + 7	14 + 8	25 + 6
36 + 5	19 + 9	24 + 8	43 + 9	17 + 4	23 + 8	15 + 9
77 + 7	45 + 9	88 + 2	39 + 3	79 + 2	28 + 9	38 + 4
38 + 6	33 + 7	35 + 7	47 + 6	88 + 8	17 + 9	88 + 9
42 + 9	39 + 5	35 + 8	87 + 3	49 + 6	87 + 3	38 + 5
58 + 3	22 + 8	36 + 4	44 + 8	64 + 9	78 + 8	34 + 8

2 digits ➕ 2 digits

regrouping

23 + 18	52 + 28	29 + 24	16 + 19	29 + 23	37 + 25	43 + 18
18 + 16	44 + 27	25 + 25	68 + 17	36 + 17	39 + 26	16 + 64
19 + 24	62 + 19	28 + 39	45 + 25	53 + 19	38 + 38	49 + 18
57 + 23	62 + 29	44 + 29	73 + 18	47 + 17	24 + 26	39 + 24
36 + 29	55 + 35	54 + 37	29 + 57	38 + 25	18 + 25	16 + 18
49 + 32	25 + 36	27 + 34	53 + 29	18 + 18	18 + 32	12 + 79
65 + 28	39 + 34	56 + 42	19 + 27	34 + 56	17 + 28	73 + 18

2 digits + 2 digits

43 + 87	59 + 46	73 + 98	77 + 35	94 + 29	77 + 45	89 + 88
35 + 86	59 + 96	67 + 66	83 + 58	54 + 98	68 + 46	79 + 79
65 + 75	53 + 89	76 + 59	84 + 39	99 + 99	78 + 47	94 + 37
99 + 88	26 + 86	94 + 96	75 + 36	54 + 89	49 + 65	46 + 57
68 + 54	27 + 86	55 + 46	53 + 99	64 + 36	99 + 78	46 + 85
58 + 78	49 + 42	75 + 37	88 + 88	35 + 75	66 + 66	37 + 64
33 + 77	69 + 44	89 + 78	99 + 47	39 + 67	57 + 88	37 + 89

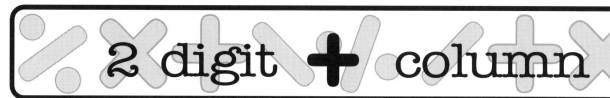
13	27	36	24	48	17	38
29	38	23	18	25	64	44
+ 17	+ 14	+ 29	+ 17	+ 19	+ 18	+ 15

12	28	15	38	19	18	38
18	25	25	42	37	19	38
+ 29	+ 37	+ 35	+ 17	+ 12	+ 25	+ 23

39	15	53	40	27	16	34
19	24	25	29	27	37	35
+ 24	+ 12	+ 19	+ 29	+ 27	+ 38	+ 18

19	28	16	53	41	16	38
19	21	25	28	16	37	27
+ 19	+ 17	+ 19	+ 15	+ 27	+ 26	+ 26

21	28	19	11	24	17	21
57	28	50	61	39	28	34
+ 18	+ 28	+ 28	+ 18	+ 26	+ 18	+ 37

46	37	22	17	15	18	25
26	26	22	26	15	29	25
+ 16	+ 18	+ 48	+ 37	+ 16	+ 70	+ 25

16	17	20	17	15	13	33
14	29	39	16	26	14	23
+ 60	+ 19	+ 39	+ 18	+ 37	+ 19	+ 34

```
   62      51      72      94      85      82      63
   74      87      78      49      66      34      75
 + 76    + 83    + 78    + 65    + 69    + 79    + 63


   78      87      93      69      77      14      56
   58      66      57      69      77      92      46
 + 98    + 92    + 72    + 69    + 77    + 95    + 98


   47      90      98      19      90      82      48
   64      60      89      92      99      94      58
 + 90    + 70    + 21    + 91    + 99    + 97    + 99


   57      93      85      75      68      67      80
   68      94      95      70      58      64      81
 + 86    + 95    + 55    + 75    + 93    + 69    + 89


   91      88      27      67      98      99      63
   98      77      85      66      94      99      75
 + 91    + 66    + 98    + 75    + 19    + 40    + 76


   76      65      60      19      75      74      59
   55      75      79      99      55      74      88
 + 89    + 85    + 62    + 84    + 75    + 64    + 72


   80      58      72      65      57      65      59
   78      67      67      70      83      67      59
 + 92    + 84    + 62    + 65    + 78    + 80    + 92
```

3 digits + 2 digits

regrouping once

132 + 48	807 + 37	118 + 34	207 + 64	453 + 27	314 + 67	743 + 38
118 + 69	537 + 39	716 + 67	429 + 55	238 + 57	524 + 46	452 + 19
458 + 35	926 + 58	357 + 24	612 + 78	145 + 19	444 + 48	227 + 66
424 + 36	836 + 44	618 + 45	573 + 19	928 + 43	229 + 68	334 + 49
252 + 38	309 + 69	627 + 47	866 + 25	219 + 52	954 + 28	449 + 13
748 + 39	324 + 36	465 + 29	508 + 78	222 + 58	278 + 19	105 + 89
344 + 49	239 + 47	938 + 57	557 + 36	865 + 18	102 + 79	246 + 38

3 digits ✚ 2 digits

regrouping twice

135 + 76	343 + 57	809 + 96	724 + 87	655 + 66	247 + 75	534 + 86
359 + 78	285 + 39	568 + 65	239 + 86	276 + 44	174 + 69	319 + 84
155 + 78	263 + 59	365 + 89	844 + 67	454 + 58	719 + 82	847 + 53
366 + 35	627 + 97	252 + 48	509 + 99	573 + 89	828 + 79	672 + 78
573 + 37	111 + 99	766 + 77	636 + 98	816 + 85	444 + 87	536 + 89
666 + 98	222 + 98	707 + 95	456 + 87	537 + 89	333 + 77	881 + 89
126 + 85	273 + 67	311 + 99	468 + 63	582 + 79	644 + 66	754 + 67

3 digits + 3 digits

regrouping

359 + 578	285 + 539	174 + 508	564 + 262	386 + 239	678 + 251
479 + 243	154 + 456	276 + 148	374 + 267	576 + 253	351 + 266
383 + 595	299 + 440	594 + 186	394 + 575	783 + 187	256 + 285
260 + 593	277 + 316	679 + 137	107 + 564	298 + 304	429 + 455
636 + 267	537 + 439	294 + 576	368 + 347	408 + 293	492 + 136
324 + 196	197 + 188	372 + 455	365 + 376	283 + 176	507 + 394

3 digits + 3 digits

regrouping

274 + 749	439 + 589	697 + 514	563 + 438	568 + 724	654 + 667
678 + 355	631 + 769	562 + 898	558 + 768	328 + 678	679 + 623
894 + 858	381 + 709	978 + 970	499 + 999	576 + 557	483 + 838
769 + 754	669 + 687	685 + 598	545 + 767	898 + 874	407 + 908
495 + 646	495 + 505	879 + 742	274 + 790	689 + 734	585 + 945
457 + 446	767 593	689 + 389	496 + 986	409 + 790	477 + 565

4 digits + 4 digits

regrouping

1,277 + 2,165	2,378 + 5,902	3,428 + 5,790	1,112 + 4,379	2,799 + 2,234
6,128 + 3,376	2,468 + 1,912	7,376 + 1,835	2,725 + 3,555	1,378 + 8,005
1,492 + 1,986	6,710 + 1,299	5,789 + 1,244	2,742 + 2,456	3,761 + 3,349
7,429 + 6,782	5,007 + 5,654	1,327 + 9,857	4,455 + 7,786	6,271 + 6,967
6,279 + 9,129	7,434 + 9,796	4,078 + 6,802	9,576 + 9,485	5,687 + 4,512
8,492 + 9,649	7,227 + 4,853	2,469 + 9,875	4,288 + 7,845	8,888 + 8,878

Multiple Digits

regrouping

12,592 + 63,748	28,097 + 11,646	42,791 + 23,489	39,482 + 32,578	59,625 + 34,674
62,496 + 58,734	50,763 + 73,089	99,876 + 99,765	73,655 + 73,957	85,656 + 65,497
32,947 + 96,534	65,084 + 74,978	47,592 + 52,408	52,961 + 87,594	42,736 + 88,459
127,486 + 457,483	307,126 + 293,485	487,692 + 255,508	370,493 + 558,647	247,876 + 537,524
274,376 + 546,985	132,074 + 678,349	237,601 + 948,709	827,621 + 746,587	987,465 + 978,645
2,742,687 + 4,837,924	7,387,420 + 6,947,798	5,547,606 + 7,568,705	1,037,098 + 9,479,394	

Review Sheet

regrouping

22	35	88	17	45	44	78
+ 8	+ 7	+ 8	+ 9	+ 9	+ 8	+ 8

49	36	55	99	27	53	64
+ 32	+ 29	+ 35	+ 88	+ 86	+ 99	+ 36

46	17	15	19	75	57	65
26	26	15	99	55	83	67
+ 16	+ 37	+ 16	+ 84	+ 75	+ 78	+ 80

440	627	866	582	573	111
+ 39	+ 47	+ 25	+ 79	+ 37	+ 99

537	260	492	685	898	689
+ 439	+ 593	+ 136	+ 598	+ 874	+ 389

2,378	7,434	42,791	487,692	1,037,098
+ 5,902	+ 9,796	+ 23,489	+ 245,508	+ 9,479,394

```
   19        46        88        43        36        28        38
  + 7       + 8       + 2       + 9       + 5       + 9       + 6
```

```
   53        18        18        78        94        39        57
  +29       +18       +32       +47       +37       +67       +88
```

```
   11        24        94        65        99        63        87
   61        39        49        70        99        75        66
  +18       +26       +65       +65       +49       +76       +92
```

```
  938       102       444       573       666       365
  +57       +79       +87       +89       +35       +89
```

```
  277       299       562       558       679       894
 +316      +440      +898      +768      +623      +858
```

```
  1,327     39,482     52,961     827,621     7,387,420
 +9,857    +32,578    +87,594    +746,587    +6,947,798
```

Final Assessment Test

| 13
+ 45 | 32
+ 37 | 15
+ 24 | 44
+ 14 | 23
+ 72 | 21
22
+ 23 | 35
23
+ 11 |

| 513
+ 64 | 24
+ 603 | 323
+ 56 | 832
+ 32 | 417
40
+ 31 | 744
32
+ 10 | 525
52
+ 11 |

| 36
+ 29 | 27
+ 34 | 57
+ 23 | 73
+ 18 | 26
+ 86 | 49
+ 65 | 98
+ 88 |

| 46
26
+ 16 | 19
50
+ 28 | 53
28
+ 15 | 41
16
+ 27 | 67
66
+ 65 | 85
95
+ 55 | 93
94
+ 95 |

| 324
+ 36 | 627
+ 47 | 866
+ 25 | 294
+ 576 | 368
+ 347 | 298
+ 304 |

| 769
+ 754 | 381
+ 709 | 576
+ 557 | 274
+ 790 | 894
+ 858 | 631
+ 769 |

| 1,492
+ 1,986 | 4,455
+ 7,786 | 42,791
+ 23,489 | 487,692
+ 255,508 | 2,987,465
+ 8,978,645 |

Basic Facts Review, page 1.

0 +9 = 9	9 +8 = 17	6 +7 = 13	5 +4 = 9	1 +3 = 4	0 +2 = 2	2 +1 = 3	9 +0 = 9	3 +0 = 3	5 +10 = 15	10's
9 +6 = 15	1 +9 = 10	7 +8 = 15	3 +7 = 10	9 +4 = 13	4 +3 = 7	5 +2 = 7	4 +1 = 5	8 +0 = 8	1 +0 = 1	0's
4 +5 = 9	2 +6 = 14	2 +9 = 11	6 +8 = 14	1 +7 = 8	4 +4 = 8	5 +3 = 8	3 +2 = 5	8 +1 = 9	7 +0 = 7	0's
10 +4 = 14	2 +5 = 7	7 +6 = 13	3 +9 = 12	5 +8 = 13	8 +7 = 15	7 +4 = 11	6 +3 = 9	6 +2 = 8	3 +1 = 4	
0 +0 = 0	2 +4 = 6	9 +5 = 14	10 +6 = 16	4 +9 = 13	4 +8 = 12	2 +7 = 9	8 +4 = 12	2 +3 = 5	7 +2 = 9	1's
8 +8 = 16	3 +3 = 6	8 +4 = 12	6 +5 = 11	4 +6 = 10	5 +9 = 14	3 +8 = 11	9 +7 = 16	5 +4 = 9	8 +3 = 11	2's
7 +3 = 10	1 +1 = 2	6 +6 = 12	7 +4 = 11	3 +5 = 8	3 +6 = 9	6 +9 = 15	2 +8 = 10	10 +7 = 17	2 +4 = 6	3's
8 +2 = 10	5 +3 = 8	2 +2 = 4	9 +9 = 18	3 +4 = 7	8 +5 = 13	2 +6 = 8	7 +9 = 16	1 +8 = 9	5 +7 = 12	4's
0 +10 = 10	9 +2 = 11	10 +3 = 13	5 +5 = 10	10 +5 = 20	1 +4 = 5	1 +5 = 6	1 +6 = 7	8 +9 = 17	0 +8 = 8	7's
9 +10 = 19	8 +10 = 18	10 +2 = 12	0 +3 = 3	4 +4 = 8	7 +7 = 14	0 +4 = 4	7 +5 = 12	0 +6 = 6	9 +9 = 18	8's

10's 10's 2's 3's DOUBLES 4's 5's 6's   9's

ANSWERS

The **Basic Facts Review** has facts arranged diagonally. This diagonal arrangement quickly identifies facts which are firm and facts which need attention.

Begin *Practice Sheets* at the level where several errors occur in a skill diagonals.

Beginning Assessment Test, page 2.

4 / 4 / +1 = 9	2 / 6 / +2 = 10	6 / 0 / +3 = 9	1 / 2 / +5 = 8	5 / 7 / +2 = 14	8 / 3 / +6 = 17	4 / 9 / +6 = 19	1 digit column no renaming
52 +24 = 76	11 +82 = 93	56 +43 = 99	70 +19 = 89	24 +24 = 48	23 / 11 / +33 = 77	35 / 23 / +11 = 69	2 digits + 2 digits columns no renaming
417 +72 = 489	513 +64 = 577	942 +30 = 972	417 / 40 / +31 = 488	523 / 23 / +23 = 569	713 / 46 / +30 = 789	224 / 132 / +111 = 467	3 digits + 2 digits columns no renaming
35 +7 = 42	88 +2 = 90	28 +9 = 37	44 +8 = 52	47 +6 = 53	19 +27 = 46	18 +25 = 43	2 digits + 1 digit / 2 digits + 2 digits renaming
68 +54 = 122	94 +96 = 190	64 +36 = 100	46 +85 = 131	53 / 28 / +15 = 96	17 / 28 / +18 = 63	67 / 64 / +69 = 200	2 digits + 2 digits columns renaming
440 +39 = 479	278 +19 = 297	509 +99 = 608	594 +186 = 780	394 +575 = 969	386 +239 = 625	472 +668 = 1140	3 digits + 2 digits / 3 digits + 3 digits renaming
2468 +1912 = 4380		1327 +9857 = 11,184		28,097 +11,646 = 39,743		5,547,606 +7,568,705 = 13,116,311	multiple digits renaming

Practice Sheet, page 3.

9	8	9	9	3	10	8
7	6	10	5	7	4	9
6	2	10	10	7	9	8
10	8	3	7	0	9	10
9	8	10	9	4	10	6
10	9	7	10	8	10	10
10	8	9	8	10	10	6

Practice Sheet, page 4.

12	16	13	17	11	18	12
16	18	13	15	16	15	13
16	13	11	19	17	18	15
15	15	17	12	14	11	13
11	16	12	18	19	16	19
14	18	19	14	12	17	12
19	18	15	19	14	18	13

Practice Sheet, page 5.

53	29	78	39	88	70	77
57	99	82	58	36	76	33
89	94	58	79	87	86	38
27	82	93	77	79	45	28
52	67	88	39	99	59	69
49	39	99	66	55	50	69
89	25	71	44	39	99	92

ANSWERS

Practice Sheet, page 6

92	99	88	27	53	35	58
89	46	79	98	76	78	79
80	79	45	45	63	87	76
77	79	48	66	86	61	88
93	58	49	85	92	99	36
89	85	59	78	99	37	28
77	76	53	49	58	88	89

Practice Sheet, page 7.

89	68	88	79	39	96	78
66	66	99	69	45	79	36
88	69	96	79	88	97	67
67	97	78	79	99	67	88
39	78	99	97	78	99	49
87	82	76	99	49	68	96
77	46	67	99	66	97	69

Practice Sheet, page 8.

87	78	69	66	99	97	69
67	96	68	68	75	99	89
78	79	68	89	98	96	99
49	55	97	36	98	99	94
67	96	77	69	58	78	79
99	98	89	38	89	39	89
67	97	67	49	87	97	79

Practice Sheet, page 9.

185	170	615	779	494	489	279
298	486	379	669	598	467	279
289	668	399	279	189	199	697
389	598	149	199	299	799	399
168	277	379	972	595	879	864
199	627	899	898	197	288	388
979	796	699	577	299	492	329

Practice Sheet, 10.

386	199	298	477	588	685	789
899	398	478	799	877	498	295
183	568	397	898	999	699	477
789	198	770	179	658	388	299
876	168	278	175	997	488	569
477	696	786	585	188	398	289
299	788	388	488	239	495	588

Practice Sheet, page 11.

639	988	579	799	378	658	996
899	498	998	997	946	878	877
668	976	799	996	895	799	849
969	677	696	887	999	678	879
968	899	768	587	895	997	387
949	979	788	467	997	667	997
696	898	699	995	999	787	989

ANSWERS

The **Section Diagnostic Tests** are specially arranged too. This arrangement helps to identify if there are still problems and which skills those problems are.

Section Diagnostic Test, page 13.

2 1 +4 **7**	4 4 +1 **9**	2 6 +2 **10**	4 4 +4 **12**	8 3 +6 **17**	9 4 +5 **18**	8 7 +4 **19**	1 digit columns no renaming
50 +42 **92**	25 +21 **46**	17 +32 **49**	46 +12 **58**	60 +28 **88**	51 +41 **92**	56 +43 **99**	2 digits + 2 digits no renaming
36 43 +10 **89**	12 14 +12 **38**	33 22 +42 **97**	12 12 +12 **36**	24 62 +13 **99**	22 22 +11 **55**	11 35 +31 **77**	2 digits columns no renaming
912 + 67 **979**	86 +111 **197**	503 + 92 **595**	323 + 56 **379**	472 + 20 **492**	313 + 16 **329**		3 digits + 2 digits no renaming
800 72 + 26 **898**	222 33 + 43 **298**	111 23 + 45 **179**	823 34 + 42 **899**	711 33 + 33 **777**	728 50 + 11 **789**		3 digit + 2 digit columns no renaming
213 424 + 262 **899**	134 412 + 131 **677**	314 372 + 312 **998**	613 251 + 132 **996**	146 212 + 320 **678**	324 433 + 130 **887**		3 digit + 3 digit columns no renaming

Review Sheet, page 12.

9	8	9	10	7	9	10
19	18	12	17	13	19	11
39	99	55	88	77	45	28
87	78	99	46	99	67	68
199	897	972	799	677	289	989
388	696	477	175	997	789	598
899	587	567	995	979	677	898

Practice Sheet, page 14.

22	33	26	20	54	21	44
41	22	33	20	45	22	31
41	28	32	52	21	31	24
84	54	90	42	81	37	42
44	40	42	53	96	26	97
51	44	43	90	55	90	43
61	30	40	52	73	86	42

Practice Sheet, page 15.

41	80	53	35	52	62	61
34	71	50	85	53	65	80
43	81	67	70	72	76	67
80	91	73	91	64	50	63
65	90	91	86	63	43	34
81	61	61	82	36	50	91
93	73	98	46	90	45	91

Practice Sheet, page 16.

130	105	171	112	123	122	177
121	155	133	141	152	114	158
140	142	135	123	198	125	131
187	112	190	111	143	114	103
122	113	101	152	100	177	131
136	91	112	176	110	132	101
110	113	167	146	106	145	126

Practice Sheet, page 17.

59	79	88	59	92	99	97
59	90	75	97	68	62	99
82	51	97	98	81	91	87
57	66	60	96	84	79	91
96	84	97	90	89	63	92
88	81	92	80	46	117	75
90	65	98	51	78	46	90

ANSWERS

Practice Sheet, page 18.

212	221	228	208	220	195	201
234	245	222	207	231	201	200
201	220	208	202	288	273	205
211	282	235	220	219	200	250
280	231	210	208	211	238	214
220	225	201	202	205	212	219
250	209	201	200	218	212	210

Practice Sheet, page 19.

180	844	152	271	480	381	781
187	576	783	484	295	570	471
493	984	381	690	164	492	293
460	880	663	592	971	297	383
290	378	674	891	271	982	462
787	360	494	586	280	297	194
393	286	995	593	883	181	284

Practice Sheet, page 20.

211	400	905	811	721	322	620
437	324	633	325	320	243	403
233	322	454	911	512	801	900
401	724	300	608	662	907	750
610	210	843	734	901	531	625
764	320	802	543	626	410	970
211	340	410	531	661	710	821

Practice Sheet, page 21.

937	824	682	826	625	929
722	610	424	641	829	617
978	739	780	969	970	541
853	593	816	671	602	884
903	976	870	715	701	628
520	385	827	741	459	901

Practice Sheet, page 22.

1023	1028	1211	1001	1292	1321
1033	1400	1460	1326	1006	1302
1752	1090	1948	1498	1133	1321
1523	1356	1283	1312	1772	1315
1141	1000	1621	1064	1423	1530
903	1360	1078	1482	1199	1042

Practice Sheet, page 23.

3442	8280	9218	5491	5033
9504	4380	9211	6280	9383
3478	8009	7033	5198	7110
14,211	10,661	11,184	12,241	13,238
15,408	17,230	10,880	19,061	10,199
18,141	12,080	12,344	12,133	17,766

ANSWERS

Practice Sheet, page 24.

76,340	39,743	66,280	72,060	94,299
121,230	123,852	199,641	147,612	151,153
129,401	140,002	100,000	140,555	131,195
584,969	600,611	743,200	929,140	785,400
821,361	810,423	1,186,310	1,574,208	1,966,110
7,580,611	14,335,218	13,116,311	10,516,492	

Section Diagnostic Test, page 26.

2 digits + 1 digit renaming
```
 19     46     88     43     36     28     38
+ 7    + 8    + 2    + 9    + 5    + 9    + 6
 26     54     90     52     41     37     44
```

2 digits + 2 digits renaming
```
 53     18     18     78     94     39     57
+29    +18    +32    +47    +37    +67    +88
 82     36     50    125    131    106    145
```

2 digit columns renaming
```
 11     24     94     65     99     63     87
 61     39     49     70     99     75     66
+18    +26    +65    +65    +49    +76    +92
 90     89    208    200    247    214    245
```

3 digits + 2 digits renaming
```
938    102    444    573    666    365
+57    +79    +87    +89    +35    +89
995    181    531    662    701    454
```

3 digits + 3 digits renaming
```
277    299    562    558    679    894
+316   +440   +898   +768   +623   +858
593    739   1460   1326   1302   1752
```

multiple digits renaming
```
 1327    39,482    52,961    827,621    7,387,420
+9857   +32,578   +87,594   +746,587   +6,947,798
11,184   72,060   140,555  1,574,208  14,335,218
```

Review Sheet, page 25

30	42	96	26	54	52	86
81	65	90	187	113	152	100
88	80	46	202	205	218	212
479	674	891	661	610	210	
976	853	628	1283	1772	1078	
8280	17,230	66,280	733,200	10,516,492		

Final Assessment Test, page 27.

The **Final Assessment Test** is arranged horizontally, by skills.

2 digits + 2 digits no renaming
```
13     32     15     44     23     21     35
+45    +37    +24    +14    +72    22     23
58     69     39     58     95    +23    +11
                                  66     69
```

3 digit + 2 digit columns no renaming
```
513     24    323    832    417    744    525
+64    +603   +56    +32    40     32     52
577    627    379    864   +31    +10    +11
                            488    786    588
```

2 digits + 2 digits renaming
```
36     27     57     73     26     49     98
+29    +34    +23    +18    +86    +65    +88
65     61     80     91    112    114    186
```

3 digit columns renaming
```
46     19     53     41     67     85     93
26     50     28     16     66     95     94
+16    +28    +15    +27    +65    +55    +95
88     97     96     84    198    235    282
```

3 digits + 2 digits / 3 digits + 3 digits renaming
```
324    627    866    294    368    298
+36    +47    +25    +576   +347   +304
360    674    891    870    715    602
```

3 digits + 3 digits renaming
```
769    381    576    274    894    631
+754   +709   +557   +790   +858   +769
1523   1090   1133   1064   1752   1400
```

multiple digits renaming
```
 1492    4455    42,791    487,692    2,987,465
+1986   +7786   +23,489   +255,508   +8,978,645
 3478   12,241   66,280    743,200   11,966,110
```

ENGLISH SERIES

The **Straight Forward English** series is designed to measure, teach, review, and master specific English skills. All pages are reproducible and include answers to exercises and tests.

Capitalization & Punctuation
GP-032 • 40 pages
and First Words; Proper Nouns; Ending Marks and Sentences; Commas; Apostrophes; Quotation Marks.

Nouns & Pronouns
GP-033 • 40 pages
Singular and Plural Nouns; Common and Proper Nouns; Concrete and Abstract Nouns; Collective Nouns; Possessive Pronouns; Pronouns and Contractions; Subject and Object Pronouns.

Verbs
GP-034 • 40 pages
Action Verbs; Linking Verbs; Verb Tense; Subject-Verb Agreement; Spelling Rules for Tense; Helping Verbs; Irregular Verbs; Past Participles.

Sentences
GP-041 • 40 pages
Sentences; Subject and Predicate; Sentence Structures.

Adjectives & Adverbs
GP-035 • 40 pages
Proper Adjectives; Articles; Demonstrative Adjectives; Comparative Adjectives; Special Adjectives: Good and Bad; -ly Adverbs; Comparative Adverbs; Good-Well and Bad-Badly.

Prepositions, Conjunctions and Interjections
GP-043 • 40 pages
Recognizing Prepositions; Object of the Preposition; Prepositional Phrases; Prepositional Phrases as Adjectives and Adverbs; Faulty Reference; Coordinating, Correlative and Subordinate Conjunctions.

ADVANCED ENGLISH SERIES

Get It Right!
GP-148 • 144 pages
Organized into four sections, **Get It Right!** is designed to teach writing skills commonly addressed in the standardized testing in the early grades: Spelling, Mechanics, Usage, and Proofreading. Overall the book includes 100 lessons, plus reviews and skill checks.

All-In-One English
GP-107 • 112 pages
The **All-In-One** is a master book to the Straight Forward English Series.
Under one cover it has included the important English skills of capitalization, punctuation, and all eight parts of speech. Each selection of the All-In-One explains and models a skill and then provides focused practice, periodic review, and testing to help measure acquired skills. Progress through all skills is thorough and complete.

Grammar Rules!
GP-102 • 250 pages
Grammar Rules! is a straightforward approach to basic English grammar and English writing skills. Forty units each composed of four lessons for a total of 160 lessons, plus review, skill checks, and answers. Units build skills with Parts of Speech, Mechanics, Diagramming, and Proofreading. Solid grammar and writing skills are explained, modeled, practiced, reviewed, and tested.

Clauses & Phrases
GP-055 • 80 pages
Adverb, Adjective and Noun Clauses; Gerund, Participial and Infinitive Verbals; Gerund, Participial, Infinitive, Prepositional and Appositive Phrases.

Mechanics
GP-056 • 80 pages
Abbreviations; Apostrophes; Capitalization; Italics; Quotation Marks; Numbers; Commas; Semicolons; Colons; Hyphens; Parentheses; Dashes; Brackets; Ellipses; Slashes.

Grammar & Diagramming Sentences
GP-075 • 110 pages
The Basics; Diagramming Rules and Patterns; Nouns and Pronouns; Verbs; Modifiers; Prepositions, Conjunctions, and Special Items; Clauses and Compound-Complex Sentences.

Troublesome Grammar
GP-019 • 120 pages •
Agreement; Regular and Irregular Verbs; Modifiers; Prepositions and Case, Possessives and Contractions; Plurals; Active and Passive Voice;

Math Series

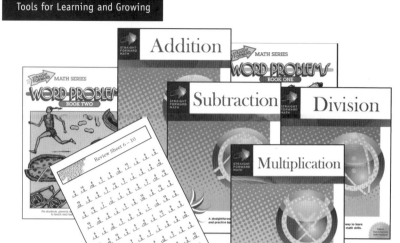

The Straight Forward Math Series

is systematic, first diagnosing skill levels, then *practice*, periodic *review*, and *testing*.

Blackline

GP-006 Addition
GP-012 Subtraction
GP-007 Multiplication
GP-013 Division
GP-039 Fractions
GP-083 Word Problems, Book 1
GP-042 Word Problems, Book 2

The Advanced Straight Forward Math Series

is a higher level system to diagnose, practice, review, and test skills.

Blackline
GP-015 Advanced Addition
GP-016 Advanced Subtraction
GP-017 Advanced Multiplication
GP-018 Advanced Division
GP-020 Advanced Decimals
GP-021 Advanced Fractions
GP-044 Mastery Tests
GP-025 Percent
GP-028 Pre-Algebra Book 1
GP-029 Pre-Algebra Book 2
GP-030 Pre-Geometry Book 1
GP-031 Pre-Geometry Book 2
GP-163 Pre-Algebra Companion
GP-168 Fractions Mastery

Upper Level Math Series

GP-104 Algebra, Book 1
GP-105 Algebra, Book 2
GP-167 Algebra Book 3
GP-045 Trigonometry
GP-054 Geometry
GP-053 Pre-Calculus
GP-064 Calculus AB, Vol. 1
GP-067 Calculus AB, Vol. 2

Math Pyramid Puzzles

Math Pyramid Puzzles
GP-162
5 two-sided puzzles

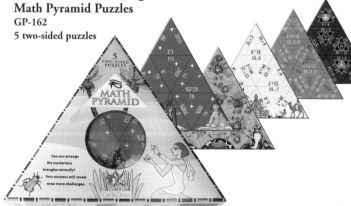

Assemble 5 two-sided puzzles each with different mathematical challenge Solve the mathematical pyramid on the front side, turn the clear tray ov to reveal a problem of logic: percents, decimals, fractions, exponents an factors.

Start building your pyramid at the bottom. The center piece is labeled and the picture may offer a clue.

Use your math skills to match sides with the same value.

You may find more than one match, but **all sides that touch** must match. When you are satisfied with your solution, close the tray.

Turn over and check the back. If the pieces are in order, you are correct!

Now, can you solve this logic puzzle?